Alcoholic,
Abusive,
Addictive
Poetry

By
Larry Bumgarner
lb060452@yahoo.com

Index

One Day At A Time

All across the world
there are people
who's today will be their last.

All the days before
are gone,
never to return,
tomorrow,
will never come.

Today,
this one singular
itty bitty day
will be all they have
their entire lifetime
of which to live.

We'll all be there sometime
one last day is all there will be,
it could be today,
who knows
what tomorrow brings.

And when it comes
and I look back
I don't want to see
that I died a lifetime
just to live for one day.

An Angel Appeared

She looked me in eye and confessed
that she had sold her body for drugs and alcohol.
And just like that,
where my angel had been sitting,
a whore appeared.
The guilt
the shame
the remorse
all told her she was unworthy of my love.
Maybe so I thought,
but not God's love
which I let flow from Him
through me
to her
unconditionally.
And just like that,
where my whore had been sitting,
an angel appeared.

Don't Quit Before The Miracle

Don't quit before the miracle
is what they told him
so he hung in there
giving it his all,
but there's a limit
to how much one can take
when everything keeps,
and continues,
to go wrong,
everything you try
comes up empty.
So he deducted
it's only a carrot,
that thing about the miracle,
dangled in front
to keep one believing
in something that isn't there,
running the razor
across his wrist
a knock on the door,
a voice yelling you've won the lottery,
you're rich!
Racing to the phone,
like him,
it was dead,
for nonpayment,
of the dues
you have to pay.

Life In The Penal Colony

No walls,
guards,
or bars
on the windows.
The jury convenes
after the prosecutor
has laid out the evidence
that I
the accused
am a loser,
unfit for success,
loving
or being loved.
I'm sentenced by my mind
and a hanging judge
to a life of loneliness,
despair,
and shame.

Doing Time

There's nothing like
the sound
when the guard
closes your cell door
a certain clang
that once you hear it
you never forget
or the feelings you have
after you've heard it
knowing that life
now exists
in an eight by ten world
and nothing you do
will get you out
the world out there
just a memory of yesterday
a dream for tomorrow
which ever you choose
it doesn't matter
there is no hope
no future
only time
which inches along
there's nothing like
the sound
when my wife comes home
closing the front door
that once you hear it
you never forget
or the feelings you have
after you've heard it.

It Just Keeps Ticking

When I awake in the morning
the Timex commercial kicks in,
you can smash it,
freeze it,
put it under water
it just keeps ticking.
I should have jerked off, flushed you down the toilet,
you'll never amount to anything,
you're stupid,
I'll give you something to cry about,
you were a mistake,
why can't you be like your sister.
You can drug it,
drown it in alcohol,
bang it against the wall,
it just keeps ticking.
The subconscious,
with no dimension of time,
doesn't know the years have passed,
playing the tapes over and over
like an eight track cassette,
always playing
never stopping
over and over
and over again

All The Fuses Are Blown

I sat there in my mind's eye and
watched as the doctor
crawled into my head
for a look around
to see what it was
that was not right.
He exited and promptly announced
that I didn't need a doctor
but an electrician,
the fuse box was all shorted out
from too much input
at such an early age
of negativity and neglect
by parents who did too much
alcohol
drugs
yelling
punishing
fighting.
The input had been too much
the surge too great
the fuses too small.

Black & White Thinking

One minute it was like driving at night without the lights on,
the next it was like driving into that low lying Winter sun that
blinds you.
One minute groping where you are
the next holding your hand up to shield your eyes.
And so quick,
from one to the other,
one moment the cranium a blue cloudless sky,
the next a raging howling storm.
How could it change so quick
from one extreme to the other?
How could I go from being all right
to being all wrong,
from so good
to so bad.

I Married The Bottle

The head trips,
fights for control,
lack of sex,
battles over money,
were easily solved,
when I divorced my wife
and married the bottle
which never gives me a hard time
dirty looks
makes me feel guilty
asks me where I've been.
It never degrades me when I look at another bottle
leans on me
cheats on me
betrays me,
just patiently waits until I get home
is there for me
always puts out
and always satisfies me.
Hasn't yet threatened divorce
has no in-laws
and doesn't expect flowers.
I can share it with my friends,
has no periods,
mid-life crisis's,
hot flashes,
or bad moods.
People tell me I'm an alcoholic,
drink too much,
should make meetings,
but I respond,
the honeymoon is still going on
the divorce would be too painful
couldn't imagine life without it
satisfies all my needs,

it's the perfect mate,
I've found my true love,
in the bottle.

On The Side Of The Road

Out of gas,
broken down,
off the road,
pulled over
on the shoulder
of life,
a lifetime of disappointments
hasn't prepared me,
doesn't ease
the feelings I have.
I can only sit,
watching everyone zooming by
lives with meaning,
going somewhere,
no one even slows down
let alone stop,
they disappear off into the distance.
It's getting late,
I wish God would send a tow truck
to salvage this wreck,
pull me out of here
give me direction
jump start me,
my life,
is broken down,
on the side of the road.

Get Over It

The past abuse was lodged deep down in my subconscious,
existing but not immediately available,
not existing, colorless, odorless, tasteless,
I could perceive it, I was aware that I wasn't right
but couldn't perceive it, apprehend it, find it.
It was not marked by thought
will, design or perception,
yet it was.
It existed, always was, always would be,
but it didn't exist, was dimensionless and timeless.
Get over it,
get over it they said to me.
But how do you get over something
you cannot see?

Name Your Poison

It starts out like a party
the first beer,
fix,
love,
feels like it will never end,
becomes intoxicating
exhilarating,
exciting,
euphoric,
you can't get enough
alcohol,
drugs,
blondes,
needing a little bit more
to sustain the high
trying to rekindle
the initial rush,
you become addicted
to vodka,
smack,
sex,
looking outward
to fulfill the inner
but it betrays you
turns against you
takes everything you have
swearing you'll never
drink,
drug,
love again,
white knuckling it
you cold turkey
shaking,
sweating,

swearing,
going through hell,
you begin to recover,
get over it,
you begin feeling,
lonely,
empty,
bored,
going back,
chasing it again
thinking it'll be different,
the drink,
drug,
woman,
gets you again,
this time
no intoxication,
exhilaration,
euphoria,
the whiskey,
coke,
females,
you name it
it's poison,
starting out as love
becomes addictive
kills you.

The Meek Shall Inherit The Grave Yard

Turn it over
Live and let live
Let it go
Turn the other cheek.
And to you I say fuck you
and you and you and you.
Niceness
is a weakness-
the predators sniff you out
jump all over you
stick the shiv
deep into my gut
letting me bleed
all over the sidewalk
emptying my pockets
so I looked him in the eye
said yeah, we'll go
right now
no problem
I just want to know
are you ready to die?
to call this day your last?
'cause I am
suicidal
homicidal
who cares
if I kill
or if I die
it doesn't matter to me
how about you?
I myself
have no reason
to live or to die
and he knew

I wasn't going to
Turn it over
Live and let live
Let it go
Turn the other cheek
so he moved back
let me pass
move on
knowing there's two people you don't mess with
one's a guy with a gun
the other's a guy who doesn't give a shit
and I was both
so take your cliches
your cute little sayings
and stick them up your ass.
I'll take my thirty-eight
my pissed off don't give a shit attitude
and we'll see
who lives
who dies
who inherits this earth.

Buried Alive

There was so much fear to let anyone in,
back off, not a step closer, go away!
If anybody got in,
saw what I could see-
all over the walls,
UNWORTHY in big capital letters,
not just written, but carved
by the fingers of a mind,
trying to escape the tomb
in which it had been buried alive,
dried blood stains under the letters,
evidence of the pain it took,
the futility of escaping,
the knowledge of being sealed in,
never getting out.
But she couldn't see it, the unworthiness,
I don't know what she was looking at,
it was right there,
but she kept on coming,
closer and closer,
causing me to panic,
I pushed her away, told her to go
staying entombed in my mausoleum,
back to inscribing my epitaph,
remaining unworthy.

It Pays No Dividends

I prayed and prayed for riches
believing
if money couldn't buy me happiness
then I was shopping in the wrong place.
If I had it I would be somebody,
have self-worth,
an identity.
The car, the house
would hide the emptiness
of my inside.
But God wouldn't deliver
so I toiled
night and day
driven to prove myself.
I made it
saved it
hoarded it
until it grew beyond my wildest dreams.
One day
I was diagnosed terminal,
the end was near.
The money,
I had it
didn't need it
couldn't use it
where I was going.
Had a resume,
but no life,
my bank account
would have to be my biography.

Hotel Pink Cloud

Time is up,
you must check out
of the hotel Pink Cloud
where not just taking a drink
is not enough.
We hope you enjoyed your stay
found the accommodations hospitable
the facilities peaceful
the rooms serene.
It was a nice stay
but now it's time to go
that time in recovery
where riding that wave of euphoria,
that pink cloud one gets when first sober
is about to come crashing down.
Your mind
denied a drink
for some time
begins with a kick start
working overtime
everything in the subconscious
becomes thoughts
igniting emotions
marked by terror, panic and alarm,
flooding, overwhelming, overrunning
inundating your mind.
The guilt of the past
the fear of the future
the shame of it all
makes me scream
what have I done?
racing faster and faster
wave after wave
it keeps coming

replaying my past
I can't catch my breath.
I pound on the door
of hotel Pink Cloud
but there's no vacancies
I can't go back
they won't let me in
the vacation is over.

Helping The Alcoholic

Having had my spiritual awakening,
cruising through life without a drink
and a Higher Power,
I stood on the deck
leaning against the rail
watching my alcoholic wife
in a panic,
splashing and wailing away
treading water trying to keep afloat.
She had gone to the bottom a few times before
and I dove in pulling her up,
dragging her to shore,
resuscitating her,
the gratitude to be alive
short-lived
the message lost
she went back to drinking again.
Those about me on the deck
screamed at me to do something
as she disappeared beneath the water
fighting to get her head to the surface again.
She gasped and fought to stay afloat
while I stood content
knowing that I too had gone off the deep end,
to the bottom,
where it finally got through,
that I couldn't swim without a life preserver,
a Higher Power to get me through,
that the drink didn't keep me afloat
it pulled me down.
Her body was now exhausted,
the struggle too tiring
she was about to go down for good
her eyes looking for me to throw a life line,

save her.
The terror on her face
building with each anxious passing moment
the people about me
ignorant about alcoholism
yelling at me to do something
one of them grabbing my arm
spinning me around
FOR GOD'S SAKE MAN!
DO SOMETHING!
SHE'S YOUR WIFE FOR CHRIST'S SAKE!
HELP HER!
I am helping her I replied,
and much to their consternation
I excused myself
as she disappeared under the water
heading to the murky depths below
where it was now her responsibility
to sink or swim
drink or not
live or die.

I Can Feel It But I Can't Touch It

Invisible yet I see it,
silent but I hear it,
I can feel it, but I can't touch it,
so subtle,
whispering,
so loud,
screaming,
I'm different,
defective,
inferior.

The Smell Of Blood

I had just been shot in the head,
kicked in the groin,
stabbed in the back…
my lungs,
had been ripped out.
She, that black widowed spider
with blonde hair
and mysterious eyes,
the love of my life,
approached and grinned.
Blood, my blood,
dripping from her fangs,
asked if I would be so kind
as to permit her to do it again.
Sorry I said, I don't think
there's any more damage
you can do,
it's all been done.
I'll be back was her reply,
when you've healed,
forgotten the pain.
She crawled back into her web,
sitting, watching, never taking her eyes off me,
so beautiful,
cunning, baffling, powerful…
patient, she'd wait.
It was something about my blood
the smell of it,
the scent,
made it all worthwhile,
turned her on.

Feelings

I wonder what it's like to feel.
I was anesthetized
as a child
the yelling
screaming
fighting
of parents who drank too much.

My emotional system
like my jaw
when I leave the dentist chair
whether it be
hurt or love
pain or ecstasy
failure or success
it all feels the same
when you're numb.

But I can feel the pain
when I look back
no novacane strong enough for that.

To get to my feelings
I must go through the pain
put it behind me
but it hurts
there
right where you're touching
and I recoil.

So here I sit
wondering
what it must be like

to feel
anything
but pain.

Why Eat If You're Only Going To Shit?

What happens to it?
where does it all go?
when God's all around
pumping out love
reigning it down
unconditionally giving it
excessively, abundantly
to everyone
free of charge
no strings attached
sucked up by human black holes
changing energy into matter
like taking food, nourishment
and producing excrement
turning love into hate.

Until Death Do Us Part

His hands,
wrapped,
tightly around my neck,
not like the times before,
when he'd stop
in the nick of time,
give me another chance,
now..
oxygen,
cut off
feeling faint
turning blue
my mind
fading out
knees
beginning to buckle
a bright light
friends beckoning me
from the tunnel
it occurs to me
I'm dying,
my life
being snuffed out
my vows
holding true
until death
do us part.

Underage Drinking

You look like you've got a keg in your belly
I could hear someone say,
the laughter, the jokes
nobody knew I heard them,
but I did, and could
hear the bartender set another beer on the bar
not even caring I was underage
or drunk already,
years later,
in meetings,
I'd hear guys say,
they had their first drink at thirteen,
hell, I was still in the womb,
had my first drink
before I was born.

To Drink or Not To Drink

The proposition was pretty much straight forward.
Quit and you live.
Drink and you die.

To most there would be no choice
because they have a choice
but when you're alcoholic you have no choice.

Unlike most I wasn't afraid of dying
for I had been dead for some time
and had grown quite comfortable in it.

The only thing missing was the embalming fluid
which I consumed day after day after day
year after year.

Waiting for the day when I would be legally dead
and all this was behind me,
the suffering the pain the loneliness.

No, it wasn't death I was afraid of,
it was the living that scared hell out of me,
the joy the love the happiness.

I trembled at the thought
as I made my decision
and hoisted that one last drink.

The Time Bomb

Everyone can hear the ticking,
their nostrils can smell the fuse burning.
Anger,
tick, tick, ticking away,
explodes in disproportion
to the hurt right now.
A small rejection,
like a detonator
sets off all the dynamite
of thirty years ago,
when the mines were laid, planted
during a childhood denied.
Erupting into rage
the explosion
wounds, maims, destroys
those closest to me,
the one's that mean the most.
I must defuse this bomb
before it kills me and my love ones,
I have to go in,
remove the detonator,
the resentments,
by forgiveness,
of a father
who raped me and my sister.

The Stray

By time the stray
found its way to me
it had changed owners
a few times.

All alcoholic owners,
who had terrorized this
poor pathetic thing
with their rage and threats.

I called and it trembled,
I offered food and it backed away,
standing and shaking
cowering in fear.

But this stray was no dog,
but the most beautiful woman
I had ever seen
who had been beaten and abused
so far into submission,
that no matter how safe I was,
or how much love I could give,
would not
could not
get close to me.

Rejected Love

I was there to deliver gifts
of love
intimacy
caring
sharing.

I knocked on her door
but spying the gifts through
the keyhole
she became enveloped
in panic
and locked the deadbolt.

I knocked and knocked
until my knuckles bled
at which time the thought
occurred to me
that I must have
the wrong address.

Time was running out.
I couldn't stay.
So as painful as it was
I departed
leaving behind
a relieved but lonely woman
to her fear and isolation
both of us confused
why my gifts she could not receive.

The Martyr

She was a martyr,
everything I said or did victimized her,
my expressions, my body language, even my gifts
affronted her, offended her standards.
Turning on me, I became the villain, and he the hero,
until one day, an innocent remark
turned him into the villain with a new hero on the way,
who rode into her life like those countless others before.
All the heroes became villains
and off they were sent
until one day there weren't any left,
no more heroes to ride in.
Lonely and loveless,
clutching to her suffering,
dying for her principles,
a martyr for the cause,
a victim,
of herself.

Betrayal

I walked the gang plank for her,
got way out on the end,
where there's no safety net,
vulnerable, exposed,
trusting, caring, giving, loving.
I laid my Self on the line,
like a ripe fruit,
dangling from the tree,
ready to be plucked,
which she did,
with a smirk on her face,
she stuck the knife right in my back,
and with her foot,
pushed me overboard,
and laughed,

as my bleeding,
attracted the sharks,
those thoughts of betrayal,
which ate me alive,
her, her, her,
every thought,
about her,
denial,
she didn't, she couldn't,
anger,
that bitch,
revenge,
I'll get mine,
Despair,
never again,
the torment,
no peace,

her weapon of choice,
baited with trust,
then poisoned,
betrayal,
the cruelest of deaths.

Because I'm A Woman

Is there something that I don't know about?
Are women endowed with some unalienable right?
Bequeathed by the highest of highs,
granted by governmental authorities.
Or is it an heirloom?
Handed down from female to female,
a defective gene maybe,
transferred by DNA.
Like it's a license
to drive
men
up a wall
off the deep end
over the edge
having refined mental cruelty
to an art.
Chameleons all,
changing from one moment to the next
never giving you an easy target
always keeping you off balance
never knowing what they want
nothing's ever good enough
everything I do is wrong.
Then looking me in the eye and saying
because I'm a woman,
which justifies it all
makes it ok
gets them off the hook.
So I tried it.
After she had me foaming at the mouth
from one of her head trips
I pulled out the axe
chopped her into little itty bitty pieces
and when they took me away

they asked me why?
So I said
because she's a woman.
But it didn't work for me,
it only works for them.
Now doing life,
which I was already was,
with her,
because she was a woman.

Alcoholism, The Lonely Disease

No food
No electricity
No gas
No telephone
No job
No wife
No kids
No friends
No respect
No worth
No honesty
No liver
No future
No body, but me and this bottle.

The Operation Was A Success

After ripping my heart out
telling me it was over
was moving on
she calls, wanting to be friends
asking me how I'm doing.
Okay I guess.
Except for the loss of blood,
the cerebral hemorrhaging,
and insomnia
I'm doing fine.
The operation was a success,
lancing that love from my life,
there'll be a few side affects I suppose.
I went down to the liquor store though,
got a bottle of anesthesia,
it's helping to ease the pain.
How about you dear?
I hope you didn't get any blood on your hands,
that was quite a hole you left,
made quite a mess.
You're drinking?
She was alarmed,
that stuff will kill you,
you shouldn't be drinking.
Shouldn't have loved either,
that'll kill you too.
But hey,
thanks for the concern,
that's what friends are for.

Take It Away

I scrubbed and scrubbed
washed and washed
but I couldn't get myself clean enough,
no soap would wash it away.
I cut and cut
but I couldn't bleed enough
to punish it away.
I cleaned and cleaned
but I couldn't obsess it away.
I ran and ran
from one man to the next
but I couldn't screw it away.
I drank and drugged
but I couldn't sedate it away.
The memories,
I couldn't take away,
of daddy,
his foot steps,
on the stairs,
up to my room,
my innocence
he took away.

Sad, Lonely and Loveless

I'm a sad man
writing sad words
living a sad life
in a sad world.
I'm a lonely man
writing a lonely poem
living a lonely life
in a lonely world.
I'm a loveless man
writing loveless stanzas
living a loveless life
in a loveless world.
I'm looking for a sad, lonely, loveless woman,
living a sad, lonely, loveless life,
in a sad, lonely, loveless world,
who doesn't want to be sad, lonely, loveless anymore.

One For The Road

I felt the hand of someone grabbing my arm
asking me if I was all right
which awoke me from my blackout.
Raising my head up from the steering wheel,
somewhere in my neighborhood,
close to home,
flashing red lights everywhere.
At first glimpse
I could see my car
imbedded into the side of another,
driven almost half-way through it.
My windshield looking like a spider web
where my head had smashed it,
the cop opened my door,
helping me out
I had to steady myself,
get my bearings.
The rescue people
were working frantically on the other car
trying to extricate someone.
Now I've really done it I thought,
wiping blood from my forehead,
leaning back against my mangled car.
I started to come around,
the fog from the whiskey was beginning to lift,
my first coherent thought
was what am I going to tell my wife
when the next thing I knew
they rolled her body by me
and then
my ten year old daughter,
putting them in the ambulance
taking them to the morgue.

Unwanted

My first drink, in the womb
as mom sucked down her gin
depressed that I was inside of her,
yeah....
I'm pregnant,
I need this like a hole in my head.
She didn't know I could hear everything,
nor see,
the expressionless look on her face
as the doctor handed me to her.

Into The Breach

She persisted,
kept coming,
physically then sexually,
which was fine,
but now she wanted to know me,
what I was thinking,
how I felt.
To your positions men!
I shouted over the din
as war preparations
were hastily made,
the enemy is at the gate!
I knew once she got in there,
got to know me,
she wouldn't find anything to love.
Bedlam broke out
as troops scurried to their positions
on top of the fortifications
I had built around my mind.
What's wrong she asked,
what's bothering you?
The screams of the wounded
and childhood memories
could be heard above the explosions
as her advancing army
tried a frontal assault upon the gates.
Let's talk about it she said,
I love you, I care.
Remember what happens if she takes us captive
I yelled, rallying the men
who flung themselves into the breach
first with shot, going with bayonets, then hand to hand
fighting like hell
sacrificing themselves

to protect the inner sanctum
of my thoughts and feelings.
We have to communicate, to talk,
without it, this relationship isn't going to work,
then she said I'm sorry, and departed.
A great roar went up from the troops,
celebrating, waving their sabers in the air.
The losses were heavy, she was a good woman,
but damage control reported back,
found the inner sanctum intact,
the defects of character saved,
the enemy had been successfully repelled.

.

I Died The Day I Was Born

My spirit
An ember
Of the fire
That is God
Having no beginning
Always having been here
Dimensionless
Perfect love
Peace
Enters into me at conception
To begin my human experience
Now constricted by time and dimensions
The ego
Reduces my spirit to a lifeless entity
With hate and anger
Greed and lust
Envy and Jealousy
Killing my spirit
Now a damp cold cadaver
John Doe
At the morgue
Waiting to be claimed
The Great I Am
Now me, me, me
I try
To resuscitate it
By prayer
And meditation
But the worldly ways
Are too powerful
My sins too many
The fleshly pursuits
Extinguish its flame
Until

One day
The heart stops beating
The lungs stop breathing
The mind stops thinking
The spirit
Free to go
No longer handicapped by the physical
It exits
And rises
Returning
From hence it came
My spirit
The Great I Am
Once again
Perfect love and peace
I died
The day I was born
And was born
The day I died

Finding Love In A Bar

I keep looking for love in a bar.
Like looking for perfume in a cesspool,
trying to buy a hammer in a linen shop,
flapping my arms to fly.

There's no love in bars,
only drunks,
sickness,
decay.

Would I look for love
in a lunatic asylum,
a train wreck,
concentration camp?

I found
plenty of husbands,
boyfriends,
paramours.

But no love.

Yet I keep going back.

Love or Insanity?

Utterly foolish,
a deranged state,
lack of understanding,
extreme folly,
unreasonableness,
unsoundness of mind..
insanity or love?
Insanity by definition,
love by experience.
Different,
yet the same.
Does anyone go out looking for insanity and find love?
No, they go out looking for love and find insanity.

Gone Fishing

I was a victim of
parents
brothers
sisters
bosses
jobs
judges
lawyers
governments
the country
world
universe
so I decided to go fishing
find a caretaker
someone to provide for me,
to do what I wouldn't.
I put the bait on the hook
helplessness
stories of abuse
physical ailments
poverty
emotional pain
a lost childhood
mental deficiencies
and cast it out there
waiting for someone to swim by.
A few sniffed the bait,
a couple nibbled,
but they were too together
to do for me what I should be doing for myself.
So I waited with the hook baited with my tales of woe,
my patience paying off
a child of an alcoholic
took it hook, line and sinker

denying himself
giving giving giving
until so exhausted he floated belly up to the top
whereupon I took him to a taxidermist,
had him stuffed and mounted putting him over the mantel.
I rebaited the hook casting it out
knowing there were more fish out there
caretakers, enablers
all too ready to be reeled in.

Extremist Thinking

All or none
black and white,
are extremist thinking
characterizing the alcoholic,
if I was to recover,
I had to stop thinking this way.
But if I was to stop drinking forever
that in itself
was extremist thinking
all or none
black and white
so I got a bottle of Johnie Walker Red
and gave the thinking a little color.

Change What You Can

What an undertaking
trying to change the entire human race
to fit my needs
quell my fears
appease my control.
I've been forty years into the undertaking
and still have six hundred billion Chinese to go,
I'm way behind schedule,
have to step it up,
to arrange it all,
to be fear free.
Compared to him, my husband,
the entire universe will be a snap
he's set me back,
starting during the honeymoon
there was no time to waste
the immovable object
he never ever got the point
could never see
that I knew what was best for him,
who he was supposed to be.
But he's now gone,
it's the world
I'm setting my sights on,
so many scripts to write,
so many people,
so many actors,
so many roles,
so little time,
my fear now
is I'll never get it done,
and with thoughts like that
how secure can I be?

COA Love

One man, one woman,
both, children of alcoholics,
trying to give love,
trying to receive love.

You're a pig she said.
You're a whore he said.
Eat me.
Blow me.
I hate you.
I hate you too.
It's your fault.
You started it.
I never want to see you again.
Ditto.

I miss you she said.
I miss you too he said.
I love you.
I love you too.
Let's not hurt each other again.
Never.

You're a pig she said.
You're a whore he said.
Eat me.
Blow me.
I hate you.
I hate you too.
It's your fault.
You started it.
I never want to see you again.
Ditto.

One man, one woman,
both, children of alcoholics,
trying to give love,
trying to receive love.

Around And Around We Go

Things were great
Conversations were witty, humorous, spontaneous
The love-making out of this world
I couldn't find a flaw in her, nor she in me
It was too good to be true
Which made me apprehensive
The anxiety of things going right
Caused me to retreat
Pull back
Which set her fears off
Blaming me
For being angry
Which I wasn't
So I defended myself
Which she interpreted me as blaming her
Putting her on the defensive
Then going on the offensive
The sooner we fight the sooner we make up
So we fought
Knock down drag out no holds barred
Going right for the jugular
Limping away
Bruised and battered
We licked our wounds
Keeping our distance
Until we made up
Apologized
Made amends
Then reunited
We made love
We fought
Made up
Reunited
Made love

Fought
Reunited
And around and around we go

The Bunker

Hunkered down in my bunker
as life's incoming
bombards my central nervous system
the Generalisimo sits at his desk reading Intelligence reports.
The light bulb sways from the explosions detonating above
casting eerie shadows
on the corkboard attached to the wall
which holds the map of my mind
that is covered with colored tacks
representing the mounting troop strength
of the ongoing assault
by the world and it's legions
which strike day and night
overrunning all sectors of my brain
overwhelming me and my thought process.
The Generalisimo stands staring at the board
wondering who they are and how they got here.
I sit paralyzed in a chair,
the shades drawn, the door locked.
The mounting bills,
broken dreams,
lost loves,
have taken their toll,
driving me inward
causing me to retreat
deep, deep down in the cranium
to the reinforced bunker below,
where the Generalisimo considers the options
of cyanide, a thirty-eight or carbon monoxide.
Having vowed to fight to the last man
I am the only one left.
I refuse to be taken prisoner
by an enemy
that takes no prisoners.

Their plan is well orchestrated and executed
taking first all material things,
blitzkrieging their way through my emotional system,
then overrunning all spirituality.
I try a surprise attack
by drinking a bottle of vodka
trying to sedate them.
Too drunk,
I'm unable to launch a counter offensive
awakening in the morning
in the dark bunker
the light bulb out
the electricity now turned off.
I try to muster what strength I have left
but to no avail,
I just can't go on.
The Generalisimo peers through the periscope
seeing that the enemy has surrounded him
cutting off supply routes and all exits of retreat.
Knowing that the time is now
he enters into his log..
all sectors are overrun and securely in the hands of the enemy,
rationale, sanity, intellect…
are all gone.
There is no hope.
As leader and Supreme Commander of this army of one
he pens his final order choosing the thirty-eight.
Placing the barrel behind his car
opting for the next world
he pulls the trigger
leaving behind a headless corpse,
of which,
no one mourns,
too occupied
fighting their own wars
to notice or care.

The Ham Radio Operator

I sit at my station
Tapping away on the ham radio
Sending out messages
SOS
This ship's going down
I need help
Can you save me?
Listening intently into the headphones
All is silent
No one returns the call.
My finger works the clicker
I think I'm losing my mind
Is there any sanity out there?
This time the airwaves are filled
With the response
Of lunatics worldwide
Drowning out all sanity.
The surge causes my radio to blow a tube
A wisp of smoke rising out of the transmitter
Causing everything to go silent
Giving me the opportunity to pour myself another drink
After years of sobriety
I have now given up hope
My ship's sitting low in the water
I chug it down and replace the tube.
Powering up, I tap out another distress signal
SOS somebody, anybody, please save me.
Is there any intelligence out there?
Any hope?
Sanity?
Please come back.
But only the lunatics come back
Overwhelming all the circuits
My radio goes up in flames

The input's too much.
The water's up to the gunnels
No one's going to save me
I'm about to drown if I don't put this bottle of vodka down.
But I can't, it's the only life preserver on board.

I Had Stepped in Shit

Over fierce objections
she had persuaded me to meet her parents
meaning she had long-term aspirations
which hadn't crossed my mind
until she showed up with matching socks and shirt
which I was supposed to wear
to impress mom and dad
whom I didn't want to impress.
Also, my mind knew they knew
I was boffing their daughter
which is why I really didn't want to go,
it was a setup-
first, matching socks and shirt,
engagement,
then marriage,
they were trying to get me,
lure me in,
set the hook.
The whole thing was phony-
mom, dad, her, the house, the scene,
my matching socks and shirt
were all phony.
Sweat poured from my underarms,
my hands trembled,
I had nothing to talk about,
there was no reason for me to be there.
Hands were shook,
names exchanged,
I was asked what I wanted to drink,
a beer please,
and was brought a cola
the whole time
dad staring at me,
I about as uncomfortable as you can get.

Then the dreaded question,
what is it do you want to be?
when it was spotted
I had stepped in dog shit
and had tracked it in across the rug,
whereupon I seized the moment,
apologizing,
excusing myself,
to clean my shoes.
Out the door
I ran like hell,
out of their yard
out of her life
out of marriage and a future of matching socks and shirts.
My fortunes,
as Buddha had said,
had changed like the swish of a horse's tail.
Back at my place,
without that woman
I turned on the football game
popped a beer and hit the couch
ecstatic over my change of luck.
I had really stepped into some shit.